Moms
Like
Christ
A Merry Heart

Sarah L. Bibler

WESTBOW
PRESS®
A DIVISION OF THOMAS NELSON
& ZONDERVAN

WestBow Press books may be ordered through booksellers or by contacting:

WestBow Press
A Division of Thomas Nelson & Zondervan
1663 Liberty Drive
Bloomington, IN 47403
www.westbowpress.com
1 (866) 928-1240

Interior Image Credit: Kaytlin Bibler Photography

ISBN: 978-1-9736-6982-1 (sc)
ISBN: 978-1-9736-6983-8 (e)

Library of Congress Control Number: 2019910102

Print information available on the last page.

WestBow Press rev. date: 08/22/2019

Dedication

I am dedicating this book to my three amazing, energetic, loving, and God-fearing children. Kaytlin, you will always be my sunshine. Noah, you will always be my hunter. Caleb, you will always be my entrepreneur. Always love and trust God. He will never let you down.

Contents

Preface

Dear Mommas,

I am so proud of you for taking some time for you. As moms we put ourselves last on the list of priorities. Our families' needs always take precedence over what we need for ourselves. Well, today you have taken the steps to do something for you. I wrote this book series with two purposes in mind: 1. To help women (moms) draw closer to God, and 2. To create an environment where the older women can mentor the younger women. This journey will not be an easy one. Satan does not want either of my intentions to be successful. He will encourage you to quit, make you feel inadequate, remind you of all your failures, and make the journey seem impossible. Don't let him win! Together we can make it through. Believe in yourself, even if it's for the first time in your life. Stay at it! Start today! You're worth it! Your family is worth it! God is worth it!

Acknowledgments

Older women likewise are to be reverent in behavior, not slanderers or slaves to much wine. They are to teach what is good, and so train the young women to love their husbands and children, to be self-controlled, pure, working at home, kind, and submissive to their own husbands, that the word of God may not be reviled.
—Titus 2:3–5 (ESV)

First, I want to thank God for using me as His vessel in writing this book. For many years I have journaled, noted, and jotted information down, and now it has been brought to completion. All praise and glory belong directly to my Lord and Savior. He directed my path and helped me to become the woman I am today. It is God who will make this book useful to the women who pick it up and diligently study it. Thank you for always guiding and leading me, Father.

Next, I want to thank my family for their patience and help as I made this book a reality. Thanks for helping with all the housework, leaving me alone so I could focus, encouraging me to keep at it and not give up, and for loving me even when I fail. To Curt, you are the man of my dreams, and I love you forever and always. Thank you for loving me right where I am and pushing me to fulfill my dreams. Thank you for being my best friend. Thank you for being a wonderful father to our children. To Kaytlin, thanks for sharing the laptop with me. Thanks for not getting upset at me when I pry into your life. Thank you for being one of my best friends. I love you always, my sunshine. To Noah, thanks for asking me about my book and helping take care of Opal, our cute little puppy. All those trips to take Opal outside and oopsies pickups don't go unnoticed. To Caleb, thank you for staying up late with me while I was typing or writing. You always asked me about my book and now you can say your mom is an author! Thanks for encouraging me all the way through.

Next, I need to thank a lot of people that helped develop me into the woman I am today. My parents, Mike and Donna Porter. My brothers, Andrew, Ben, Daniel, and Isaac. Sorry for all the times I beat you up and told Mom you were the guilty one. To my sister, Anna Turner, for taking the leap of faith to become an author so I would know what to do. To my best friends for life, Katrina Groce, Annette Troyer, and Amber Grant. You ladies have inspired me more than you will ever know. Your unconditional love, helping talk through frustrating times, letting me cry on your shoulder, and leading me to God's Word not only have helped me, they have helped my family survive.

Thank you to Jenn Hemlinger, Amber Grant, and Katrina Groce for proofreading and showing me love all the way through this journey.

I would also like to thank both sets of grandparents, Don and Janet Peters and Nolan and Wilma Porter. You each created the spiritual inheritance that helped build my foundation in the right spot. I miss you, and I'm looking forward to worshiping together in heaven one day.

Introduction

The job of being a Christian mother is very intense and overwhelming. She must not only see to the physical needs of her children, she must stay aware of the psychological, social, and spiritual needs of each child. While being alert to all these conditions, she must keep the house clean, complete tons of laundry, satisfy her husband's needs, maintain a social life of her own, and keep her sanity. Moreover, some energetic mothers have a job outside of the home. Feeling overwhelmed yet? Me too!

When we become mothers, our children are a blessing from God.

> "Children are a heritage from the Lord, offspring a
> reward from him." Psalm 127:3 (NIV)

We, along with our husbands, are called to raise our children according to God's Word.

> "Start a child off in the way he should go, and even when they are
> old they will not depart from it." Proverbs 22:6 (NIV)

> "Fathers, do not exasperate your children; instead bring, them up in
> the training and instruction of the Lord." Ephesians 6:4 (NIV)

As we run the race set out before us, we will encounter God in so many different aspects of our life. God reveals Himself in and around us as long as we continue to watch for Him. We will hear stories from our parents, grandparents, and great-grandparents. Many of these stories may include revelation of God working in the lives of our ancestors. We should cherish these stories. These are what I call faith builders—experiences we use to increase our faith and trust in God.

God calls the older women to help lead the younger women (Titus 2:3–5). We older women have experienced many different seasons of motherhood. Through each season, we struggle to make daily decisions that will help equip our children for life in this ever darkening world. As young women, open your hearts and ears to the older women God has placed in your life. As older women, pray and seek God's will for using your stories to help encourage and uplift others.

Every story in the Bible leads us to a deeper understanding of who God made us to be. As mothers, we search His Word to discover the best ways to raise our children. God has so graciously given us guidelines, but how do we draw the connections between motherhood and His Word? That's what this book is all about: taking God's Word and the lessons therein and applying them to our lives. Join me on this journey as we study God's Word. We will focus on fourteen godly traits of a mother:

Book 1: A Merry Heart

Massive prayer life
Order to chaos
Merry heart
Sacrificial love

Book 2: Emotional Wreck

Loves unconditionally
Insight into our children's lives
Keeps the faith
Emotional wreck

Book 3: Super Mom

Contentment
Holds true to God's Word
Release children to God
Inspired by others
Super mom
Trust in God

As we study each of these attribute, we will relate it to different women from the Bible. Some of our examples are true godly women who lived their lives to please God. Others are women who knew of God but never took the time to draw close to Him. We can learn from each of these types of women. Every word in the Bible is for our growth as Christians. Join me on this adventure—you won't regret it.

It's about a relationship,
not about a religion.

Before starting into this book, I have an extremely important question to ask you: "Do you have a relationship with Jesus Christ, or do you have religion with Jesus Christ?" Some of you may ask, what's the difference? Aren't they the same thing? Well, I'm here to inform you they are very different from each other.

When driving through any town or city in America, you see different denominations of churches: Methodist, Catholic, Church of God, Church of the Brethren, Mennonite, Lutheran, and more. There are even churches that claim to be nondenominational. What does denomination actually mean?

> *Denomination: a religious organization whose congregations
> are united in their adherence to its beliefs and practices.[i]

Basically, denominations of churches have their own religious acts that govern their beliefs about God. Let's relate it to something most of us are familiar with—food. I prefer tacos myself, so let's start there. One denomination may say that the members of their congregation may choose to use hard or soft taco shells. Another denomination may choose only soft shells. While another denomination may use only whole wheat soft shells. You see, each denomination has created rules and/or regulations for their members based on human understandings of the scriptures. Some denominations base their beliefs and/or regulations off of more than just God's Word. They use other writings to govern their members actions. Denominations set up the way the church will run or be run by those who are a part of its churches. This is what makes up Christian religions in the world. Religions are dictated by the opinions of their leaders or developers (men and women).

> *Religion: a personal set or institutionalized system of
> religious attitudes, beliefs, and practices.[ii]

Religion is based on a human's interpretation of God's Word, which sets the boundaries and rules for those who live out its belief.

*Relationship: the state of being connected.[iii]

A relationship is actually a real connection. We all have relationships with those we call family and friends. Some of our relationships are wonderful. Wonderful relationships bring happiness, joy, love, support, peace, and tranquility to those involved. The connection of these individuals is strong and healthy. Other relationships are destructive. Destructive relationships bring sorrow, pain, hurt, unruliness, and discomfort. Unfortunately, we all may have destructive relationships in our lives too.

I want to ask you my original question again: "Do you have a relationship with Jesus Christ, or do you have religion with Jesus Christ?" If you have a religion with Jesus Christ, you have rituals you follow that are based on your church and/or beliefs. I am not saying that your religion is wrong. As long as it is based solely on God's Word, you are doing exactly what God would want you to do. If your rules or regulations are not found in God's Word, then your religion is void. It is a waste of your time to perform. God calls us to live like Jesus Christ, His Son. Either way, whether your religion follow's God's Word or not, it is simply religion.

God calls us to have a relationship with Him; a connection between us and Him. Have you asked Jesus into your heart? If you have, you should have experienced a change in your life. When we begin a relationship with Jesus, others see a change in our life as a reflection of Him. If you have not experienced a change in your life, then you have not truly begun a relationship with Him.

If you want to gain anything from this book, you must have a true life-changing relationship with Jesus Christ. You must ask Him to forgive you from your sins, to come into your heart, and to find a home within you. But this isn't the end. Next, you must seek to change from your past. The sins that Jesus has forgiven you for can no longer be a part of who you are. A true relationship with Jesus results in real change in your life. How will you know if you have truly changed? Others will see this change in you. You will not be saying the same words you used to say. You will not be visiting the same places you visited before. You will be a new person in Christ.

Before beginning this Bible study, take a few moments to talk to God. Ask Him to forgive you for the sins in your life. Ask Him to reveal His truth to you. As you wait on Him, the Holy Spirit will reveal areas in your life in which you need to make changes. Recognize these areas and strive to find out how to make these changes in your life. Remember, no one will be a perfect Christian. Jesus was the only perfect Christian on earth. God doesn't call us to be perfect. He calls us to strive for perfection. As long as we are striving to please Him in all that we do, He will continue to reside within our souls and lead us through life.

Now get ready to grow with me! God is ready and waiting! Let's not delay!

Make a Commitment

Let's start this study with a commitment statement. A promise to ourselves, our fellow bible study participants, and to God. Read and put your name in the commitment line below.

I, _____, am ready to dive into God's Word to discover, practice, and use the skills He has prepared for me. I pledge to spend time searching in God's Word, talking to God, listening to His leading, and sharing my knowledge with others in my class. I won't quit when it gets tough. When discouraged, I will refocus and continue to stay at it. I want to grow in my relationship with God so I can be the mother God has called me to be.

One of the most important attributes of this Bible study is trust. Trust between you and every other participant in the study. Many of the conversations that will take place during the next few months will involve difficult topics. It is most imperative that you remain a faithful, trusting friend throughout every conversation that occurs within all aspects of this class. I encourage you to create a text message group for support and sharing throughout the week. Support doesn't have to be limited to the times you gather together weekly. Support and prompting throughout the week can also help you each grow as mothers and children of God. Being able to trust the members of your class will not only help you share truth but will allow other women in your class to feel comfortable to share their own truths. Before the end of this study, you will have developed deep relationships with these new sisters in Christ, one that will last a lifetime.

If you vow to keep all discussions with these beautiful women confidential and are willing to be vulnerable with them, please sign the confidentiality line below. Breaking this vow will not only cause pain to the women who trust you, it will also cause pain to God. He takes your commitments and vows extremely seriously.

_____   _____

Confidentiality signature   Today's date

Mapping God's Word

Spending time with God daily is a top priority in this Bible study. Prayer is a major communication tool we can use to build our relationship with God. God has given us His Word to guide us through making major and minor decisions in life. The Bible is filled with promises, warnings, and stories that we can use to become more like Him.

Prayer is a very important part of communication with God. It is our way to let God know about us on so many levels. Our prayer life should incorporate time rejoicing and praising Him for all that He has so graciously given us, from our homes to the food on our table to our families to our jobs and so much more. Just thinking about all He has blessed me with builds within me an overwhelming desire to humbly fall on my knees and praise Him with all that I have. There are so many things in my life that I can be thankful for.

Another part of our prayer life should be seeking His will for our lives. Every day we make life decisions that reflect who we are, who we want to be, and what truly matters in our lives. Ask God to reveal to you His truths. Ask God to show you all that He has for you. Seek Him with all that you have within you.

The last but most important part of prayer is listening. God will speak to us in so many different ways. In my life, God has spoken to me through the voices of other people, billboard signs, the actions of those around me, and more. We must be diligent as we wait for Him to speak. Do I believe that God can speak to us audibly? Yes, I do. But there are so many other ways He will speak to us as well. Don't lose heart if you don't hear from Him. He is there. Just be patient, wait, and watch.

God's Word is our number one, most important communication tool. This is where we learn about Him. The only way we can become better wives, mothers, daughters, and friends is to know God more. God is all knowing. He is the author of life. He has equipped each of us with the ability to know Him on a personal level. He will not force you to grow deeper with Him. You must take the initiative to get to know Him on your own. Pick up the Bible and read it. Don't read it to just say you've read His Word. Read it to learn, grow, and understand Him.

I would like to introduce to you a process I use while reading the Bible. I call it mapping God's Word. This process helps me to grow deeper instead of just reading the scriptures. Every word God has placed in the Bible is there for a reason. If we just read the words but don't dig deeper, we may miss out on so much truth that He placed there for us. I will teach you how I use this mapping process. You can mirror my mapping, choose to use only parts of it, or use your own method. As long as you are reading scripture to grow deeper, any method will work.

Step 1: Choose which Translation You Prefer

One of the first things you need to do is to choose which translation of the Bible works best for you. There are many different translations out there. I'm old school when it comes to God's Word—I want a Bible I can hold in my hand. However, I know many women who use their phone or iPad with a downloaded app to read. Use whatever works best for you. I use the New International Version (NIV). When I graduated from high school, my church gave me a Bible as a gift. This Bible used the NIV translation. So I've just continued to use this translation to this day. In the last few years, I was introduced to an amazing website called Blue Letter Bible[iv]. This also comes as an app. The app comes with several free translations included, but you can download other versions of the Bible too. This app is amazing. You have access to Bible dictionaries, thesauruses, concordances, commentaries, videos, and so much more.

If you know of a good Bible app, be sure to share it with your Bible study group.

Step 2: Copy the Scripture into Your Book

Next, rewrite the scripture word-for-word. See my example below for week 1. (This is also found in the appendix.)

"And pray in the Spirit on all occasions with all kinds of prayers and request. With this in mind, be alert and always keep on praying for all the Lord's people." Ephesians 6:18 (NIV)

Step 3: Map out the Verse

Next, I go back to the verse and map it out. These are the guidelines I have found that help me to visually see the verse. I'm a visual learner. Highlighters are my best friends. Don't feel obligated to map as I do. Use what works best for you.

Highlight what stands out
Box a promise to proclaim
Circle words to define
Underline any commands
X OUT any sins to stay away from

"And pray in the Spirit on all occasions with all kinds of prayers and requests. With this in mind, be alert and always keep on praying for all the Lord's people."

Step 4: Define Words

Use a Bible dictionary or concordance to look up definitions of any words you may have circled. The website or map I mentioned earlier has a dictionary and concordance. What I love about a concordance is the ability to look up the Greek (original version of the Bible). We can learn a lot about God's Word by going back to the original version. You may be surprised by the many different definitions of words that we use in the English language. This helps us gain a deeper understanding of God's Word. There are various Bible dictionaries, concordances, and thesauruses. Seek out what works best for you.

Step 5: Add Commentary Notes

Commentaries are created by men or women who have studied the Bible and then lay out what these scriptures mean to them. Now, remember this is person's opinion of God's Word. So be sure to look up the Greek to compare to what others have to say. You can also use the internet to research the meaning of the verse. Just be cautious of where you are gathering these commentaries from. Be sure they are trustworthy, parallel with the Greek version of God's Word, and parallel with your pastor(s) teachings. See my commentary for Ephesians 6:18 in the appendix.

Step 6: Summary

After searching deeper, summarize what this verse means to you. Here is my summary of Ephesians 6:18:

In all circumstances pray. Even when I'm not sure how or what to say—pray. Pray for all those around me as well. Pray with those around me. Never stop praying.

Step 7: Apply It to Your Life

Write out how this verse can be applied to your life. Each time I read over a verse, I can apply it to my life in different ways. Remember that each part of God's Word is applicable to our lives. It's okay if this verse is challenging for you. It's okay if you're not sure how to apply this verse in your life. Just write from your heart in full honesty. Here's how I applied Ephesians 6:18:

No matter what I am facing—joy, tribulation, happiness, unforgiveness, anger, sorrow—go to God and pray. Prayer is one of my major communication tools with Him. If I lack talking to God, it's my fault. I need to prioritize my life to make sure prayer is a part of it.

Step 8: Pray It Back to God

From the knowledge you have gained, you now have a plan of action to apply this verse to your life; talk to God about it. Be thankful. He will lead you to these truths. Be willing to make a change in your life to live by His Word. Be open to whatever He has for you beyond what you have gained from this study. Be open and honest with Him. Here is my prayer to God after my study with Ephesians 6:18:

God, forgive me for lacking in my communication with you. I love You. I admire all I see You do in my life and in the lives of those around me. You are my one desire. I need You in my life. I can't make it through without You. Thank You for Your leadership. Thank You for Your love. Thank You for *meeting me right where I am every time I need You. You are my Savior, and I adore You!*

Now as I said before, use any part of this mapping process as you wish. Modify it to meet your needs. Skip what you do not find valuable for your studies. Add things that help you along. This process is just a guide. Do what you need to do to make it work for you.

I have included space in the book for you to map scripture. However, it may not be enough space for you to journal. Do not limit your studies and findings to the empty spaces in this book. You may want to purchase a separate notebook to complete your maps. Discover what works for you and go with it. Remember the deeper you dig into His Word, the closer to God you become.

Chapter 1

Massive Prayer Life

This is the confidence we have in approaching God; that if
we ask anything according to his will, he hears us.
—1 John 5:14 (NIV)

Day 1: Massive Prayer Life

As mothers, we never run out of worries. Will we outlive our children? Will our children get cancer or become very ill? How will our children deal with peer pressure? Will they ever sleep through the night? Will *I* ever sleep through the night again? How will they treat me when I am older? We are constantly filled with questions, always wondering what if … and how will … A mind is a scary place—a very scary place for some of us. Our thoughts can lead us to worry, frustration, and major anxiety, which are forms of bondage to Satan. It's time we clear our minds of this paralyzing struggle.

What do we need to do to fight back when Satan has taken over our thoughts? Seek God! Cry out to Him from the depth of our hearts. Tell Him about our worries and fears. Spend time on our knees.

> I pray that the eyes of your heart may be enlightened in order that you may know the hope to which he has called you, the riches of his glorious inheritance in his holy people, and his incomparable great power for us who believe. That power is the same as the mighty strength he exerted when he raised Christ from the dead and seated him at his right hand in the heavenly realms. (Ephesians 1:18–19)

When you begin to seek God to find peace, be ready for Satan's attacks. Memorizing scripture will help you stand against him. God is more powerful than Satan. Read that again. *God is more powerful than Satan!* Use God's Word to defeat Satan. Pray scripture. Post sticky notes of scripture around your home, in your car, and at your workplace. Put His Word at the forefront of your mind. God created us to be able to defeat Satan, and His Word is our number-one weapon of defense.

Our second weapon of defense is prayer. God calls us to pray in the Spirit. What does this mean? The Spirit is the Holy Spirit. When we accept Jesus as our Savior and ask Him into our hearts, we are given the Holy Spirit as our guide. When Jesus ascended to heaven, God sent us a gift: the Holy Spirit. He fulfills the Trinity: God, Jesus, and the Holy Spirit.

What is a spirit? This opens a door to some differing opinions. I believe a spirit is the soul within us. Our spirits guide our emotions and thoughts that lead to our actions. God's Spirit, the Holy Spirit, is a gift from God. His Spirit influences our spirits (our souls). Of course, the Holy Spirit is always right. He will never lead us toward evil desires or sinfulness. He is also equipped with amazing fruits. These fruits are gifts from God to help us endure our time here on earth.

> But the fruits of the Spirit is love, joy, peace, forbearance, kindness, goodness, faithfulness, gentleness, and self-control. Against such things there is no law. (Galatians 5:22–23)

These fruits are all based on positive feelings and actions. Our flesh does not naturally fall into these categories. Satan wants us to focus on the negative this world has to offer. Satan wants us so overwhelmed with negativity that we can't hear the Holy Spirit speaking truth against his lies. When we pray in the spirit, we allow the Holy Spirit to enter our minds. As we quote scriptures, the Spirit reminds us that He is more powerful than Satan. So the lies of Satan begin to break apart and we welcome in the fruits that will lead us to hope. This is just the beginning of praying in the Spirit.

I give God praise for the intervention of the Holy Spirit in my life. Even when I don't know what to pray or know how to put my needs into words, the Spirit intercedes for me. He takes my request straight to Jesus, our loving Savior sitting at the right hand of God, our Father. Wow! Talk about a highway to heaven! And we have access to this all day every day!

So what does this type of prayer life look like?

These are the moments your knees hit the floor, your heart is completely broken, and your mind is 100 percent on God. You may speak audibly or only within your spirit. Your words may not even make sense to you or those around you. During these moments, the Spirit surrounds you, inside and out. You begin to feel an unexplainable and overwhelming peace. As you cry out to God, the Holy Spirit interprets your groans for words to Jesus. Sometimes after experiences like this, you may not know or even understand what happened. Other times, you can't explain what happened, but you know God is working on your request. Sometimes it's hard to admit you don't know how to pray or what exactly you should say or ask God. Don't overthink the situation. Just fall humbly before Him.

How many of you have a fear of praying? Well, at least praying out loud? I totally get it. For many years, I worked with an amazing, God-filled family. All of them could just start praying and talking to God in such a way it almost intimidated me. When called upon to pray, I always felt like my prayer was so minimal—almost childlike.

Eventually, I choked up the nerve to talk to the momma of the family, and her words brought clarity to my life. She told me to start by praying to God out loud all by myself. She told me prayers are a communication between God and me. She encouraged me to begin to pray out loud with her by my side. She helped me to realize that no one's prayer is superior to another person's prayer. Satan wants us to feel intimidated and defeated. But if we give in to his intimidations, we continue to hold on to the things we need to release to God. I will never forget her words of wisdom.

How many of you have experienced the presence of God while praying? Take time to jot down any experiences you have to share with your group. And if you haven't had these experiences, trust me: you will. Don't lose faith. Read James 4:10. It's a promise!

I have experienced unexplainable moments with God. I recall one time when I was praying for my third child, Caleb. I already had two amazing children, but I had also experienced two heart-wrenching miscarriages. In fact, I had just experienced my second miscarriage three months prior to seeking God about Caleb. I was devastated. I struggled with wanting another child but believed I couldn't get pregnant again and face the tragedy of losing another little one. I fell before God at the altar at my church. Many friends were surrounding me and praying. My face was buried in the carpet. My eyes were filled with tears. And no words would come from my mouth. I just cried.

I began to remember scriptures of promises from God, but my mind fought those promises with lies—lies from Satan—right there at the altar in my church! And then I started quoting Jeremiah 29:11. "For I know the plans I have for you declares the Lord; plans to prosper you and not to harm you; plans to give you a hope and a future." Over and over, I prayed this scripture to God. Then I cried the word *hope* over and over again. A warm sensation came over me.

I have no idea what happened next because I literally felt like I was in the arms of Jesus. I had no worries, no anxiety, no impatience, no regret, and no pain. It was amazing.

I left that altar with a feeling of renewed hope. No, I wasn't pregnant immediately. Yes, I still had my moments of doubt. But I was always quickly reminded of Jeremiah 29:11 and hope. I plastered that verse in my house, in my car, and on my desk at work.

Eventually, God blessed me with my third child. And I will forever be grateful for that moment at the altar. As I fell humbly before God, He drew near to me.

Now you may not always have an experience like mine. God has plans for you that are different from mine, and that's okay. Don't underestimate yourself, though. God hears the prayers of a faithful servant. Always seek Him first in all things, even when you don't feel that closeness to Him. He is still near—always near.

> We know that God does not listen to sinners. He listens to the godly person who does his will. (John 9:31)

> For the eyes of the Lord are on the righteous and his ears are attentive to their prayer, but the face of the Lord is against those who do evil. (1 Peter 3:12)

Remember: God hears the prayers of the righteous. If you feel distant from God, continue to cry out to Him. Ask Him for forgiveness. Never underestimate the smallest of sins. This world levels sins into small, medium, large, and extra large. In God's eyes, they are all the same. Daily confess your sins to God. Ask Him to forgive you. If you find yourself seeking forgiveness for the same sin over and over, you may want to seek out someone to help you overcome this sin. God calls us to strive for righteousness. Never settle for less.

Spend some time in prayer this week. Ask God to reveal to you repeatable sins in your life. Seek help from a friend, counselor, elder, or pastor. Show God you are sincere about forgiveness and living a righteous lifestyle. And above all else, don't believe Satan's lies. God will forgive you.

Day 2: Mapping God's Word

(See my example in Appendix A)

Ephesians 6:18
Write It Down and Map It Out

Define Words, Thesaurus, and Commentaries

Summary

Apply It to Your Life

Pray It Back to God

Day 3: Mapping God's Word

(See my example in Appendix A)

Philippians 4:6–7
Write It Down and Map It Out

Define Words, Thesaurus, and Commentaries

Summary

Apply It to Your Life

Pray It Back to God

Day 4: Mapping God's Word

(See my example—Appendix A)

Romans 8:26–27
Write It Down and Map It Out

Define Words, Thesaurus, and Commentaries

Summary

Apply It to Your Life

Pray It Back to God

CHAPTER 1 REVIEW

Day 1: Massive Prayer Life

How is your prayer life? How much time do you spend daily in prayer to God? Do you seek Him only when you have a need? Do you take time to praise Him for all He has blessed you with? Think about the answer to all these questions and then rate your prayer life according to the rubric below:

- 5: Every second of every day I am communicating with God.
- 4: In every situation I face, I say a prayer (even if it's a quick prayer) that will lead me. I also spend time praising Him every time His blessings come to mind.
- 3: Yes, I pray to God. It's not always. Sometimes I speak or act before talking to God first. I give Him praise, but not all the time. I'm busy.
- 2: Pray? Uh, sure. Definitely not all the time—more like when I need something, or I'm super angry, sad, or frustrated. He knows I'm thankful for my blessings. I thank Him when I'm at church or when someone reminds me too.
- 1: Prayer life? What's that?

Explain why you chose the choice above:

Be ready to share your experiences with prayer that you wrote about on page 16.

Are there changes you need to make to your life to improve your communication with God? Do you pray intently or out of obligation?

Day 2 through 4: Mapping God's Word

Pick one of the verses from this week to share with your class. Pick the verse that spoke the most to you. Look back over your map for this verse. Be prepared to share how you have applied or plan on applying this verse to your life.

Write this verse in the memory verse slot for chapter one in Appendix 3. Study the verse over the next several weeks. Hide His Word in your heart. Memorize.

Chapter 2

Eunice

I am reminded of your sincere faith, which first lived in your grandmother,
Lois and in your mother, Eunice and I am persuaded now lives in you also.
—2 Timothy 1:5 (NIV)

Leaving a Legacy of Faithfulness

Eunice, the grandmother of young evangelist Timothy, is known for her legacy of faithfulness. Paul makes references to Eunice and her mother, Lois, as women who lead their children in the legacy of believing and trusting in the ways of the Lord. Eunice, a Jew, was married to a Gentile, but there is very little mentioned about her husband in the scriptures. I wonder what the circumstances must have been for her to marry outside of her faith. Since scriptures don't share much about him, he may have been a believer. Either way, Timothy was given a Jewish name, which means "one who fears God." How excited they must have been when they saw Timothy follow alongside such a godly man as Paul. It was Paul who lead this family into the knowledge that Jesus was the Messiah spoken about in the Old Testament scriptures. Paul leads the whole family to Christ and then mentored Timothy to become the youngest evangelist in scriptures.

Day 1

- **Acts 16:1–5: Timothy found by Paul**
  - o Paul, an amazing man of God, had experienced much change in his life. First starting out as a Christian man hunter, Jesus changed him into a

wonderful and powerful leader. Paul encounters Timothy through his travels.

- o Verse 1: Paul refers to Timothy as a _____. Timothy's mother was a believer, but his father was a _____.
- o Verses 2–3: Paul ask Timothy to accompany him and Silas.
  - The last time Paul was in Lystra, the people had wanted to stone him. But God saved Paul. Timothy had learned of the legacy Paul had built. He must have been extremely honored to be asked by Paul to follow Him.
  - Why did Paul circumcise Timothy?

- o Verses 4–5: According to these scriptures, how successful was these three gentlemen's ministry?

  - Knowing the kind of man Timothy was developing into, what can we infer about his mother, Eunice? Why can we make these assumptions? What about his father?

Day 2

Paul took Timothy under his wing and mentored him. Timothy must have been quite a man of God. Paul entrusted him to share God's Word in areas of the world that were completely overtaken by Satan's schemes. One Timothy and 2 Timothy are letters Paul wrote to young Timothy. These letters include instructions on the life of the local church and how to preach the message of salvation to all people. Paul warns Timothy of false preachers and teachers. He explains how to set up a church with elders and deacons. Paul describes how to use our God-given gifts, reminding Timothy there is a constant battle between flesh and the spirit. Paul had a lot of faith in Timothy and taught him so much about the church. We find in the verse below a little bit of why Paul believed in Timothy so much.

- **2 Timothy 1:5: Paul refers to Timothy's legacy in his mother and grandmother.**
  - Rewrite this verse below:

    - What does this verse mean to you?

- Describe your legacy. Was there someone in your life to whom you can trace your faith? Share a little about his or her story and how it has impacted your life.

Day 3

- **2 Timothy 3:14–17: Paul encourages Timothy to remember and share all that he was taught.**
  - Verse 13: What was Paul referring to when he said, "What you learned and have firmly believed in"?

  - Verse 14: What was Paul referring to when he said, "Knowing from whom you learned it"?

  - Verse 15: What was Paul referring to when he said "sacred writings"?

  - Verse 15: Paul refers to the sacred writings as what made Timothy wise through faith in Christ Jesus. What sacred writings have you encountered that have helped build your faith in Christ Jesus?

o Verses 16–17: What does this verse mean to you? (Look deeper by searching word definitions (in Greek), text commentaries, and more. Then make a decision for yourself on the meaning applied to your life.)

Day 4

- **2 Timothy 4:1–5: Timothy is ready**
  o What do these five verses mean to you? Do they apply to us today? In what way?

CHAPTER 2 REVIEW

1. Did our character this week have a relationship with God? If so, describe that relationship. Include any changes that may have occurred with this relationship.

2. Describe Eunice's character. What can we learn from her about faith, love, marriage, being a mother, grief, strength, perseverance, and more?

3. List an example of how this woman handled a specific struggle. Pay attention to details. These details help teach us right steps verses wrong steps to take.

4. What can we learn about being a wife or mother from Eunice's story?

Chapter 3

Order to Chaos

But everything should be done in a fitting and orderly way.
—1 Corinthians 14:40 (NIV)

Day 1: Order to Chaos

If you have ever been to my house on an unannounced visit, you have seen chaos. Clothes laying everywhere, dog toys all over the place, shoes here and there, the kitchen table is covered with who knows what, dishes piled high, and the list goes on. I purchased a sign that sits in my living room. It says, "Excuse the mess, my children are making memories." However, some days I think it should say, "I was just too tired to do anything today." Life gets busy and chaos becomes the norm. Kids have sports practices and games. You have work to do in and out of the home. You must plan meals either in advance or in the moment. There are birthday parties to plan, bills to pay, dishes and laundry to wash. Where does all the time go in a day? There are too many things to do and not enough time to get them done in.

Is there anyone with me? I know I'm not alone in this. We all live busy lives. We try to balance everything all at one time and then nothing gets done. Have you had that moment when the doorbell rings and your heart begins to race? You are hoping it is someone who already knows your life is too crazy to be organized! Then when you reach the door, it is the mailman, who is already aware of the chaos you call life.

Listen, ladies—slow down and smell the roses (or dirty diapers—whatever is your case). I have another sign in my living room that says, "Never get so busy making a living that you forget to make a life." Yes, this probably is referring to working too much. However, it reminds me to enjoy the season I'm in because one day my season will change. This busyness of life will become a desolate desert with rolling tumbleweeds. And I will wish for these busy days back once more.

So first off, you are going to have to come up with some form of organization. *Don't stop reading yet*. I'm not going to encourage you to create an elaborate plan to keep your house spotless. Here are some hints that I used with my family or examples I saw in my friends' homes. These all work, but you must make each fit your family.

1. Chores list:

    a. Dishes. We rotate the dishes among us all (except Curt—but he still helps now and then). We have a whiteboard with our monthly calendar. We took a small section and wrote down our rotation. Beside the list is a large circle. After taking your turn, you put the next person's name in the circle. If you do the dishes and forget to change the name, you have to do them again. My kids came up with that last rule because I always forget to change the name on the board.

    b. Laundry. When the kids were younger, I did all the washing of the laundry. They had to fold and put their own clothes away. This didn't always work out as I planned, but I kept at it anyway. As they grew, they had to start doing their own laundry—wash, dry, and fold. Sometimes I take time to wash everyone's laundry and then just separate each person's clothes into their own basket. Either way they have to fold and put their own clothes away.

   c. Cleaning. I'll just be honest. Since I work outside of the home, we hire a cleaning lady. Right now, my daughter is our cleaning lady. We do pay her to clean each week. But when she's busy with her school schedule, I have a friend who will clean my house for me. She does a great job, and I love helping each of them out financially.

2. Pets: The kids have their own pets, which they must take care of 100 percent. They even help purchase feed and any equipment needed for them. We also have steers in the barn. Noah usually helps Curt take care of those (Noah works on the farm for Curt, so this goes along with his job). We are always having new and different pets in the barn—goats, sheep, rabbits, cats, chickens, turkeys, and who knows what else. If the kids want to have pets, they must help take care of them.

   a. Not everyone is a pet person, but we have used pets to help teach our children responsibility. It has proven very successful. On more than one occasion, we have had to find new homes for pets because our kids didn't hold up their end of the bargain. This broke hearts but lessons were taught.

3. Allowance: Everyone has their own ideas about whether their children should earn allowance or not. So here's our philosophy. We want our children to learn how to save, budget, tithe, and spend wisely. When we give them extra little jobs to do around the house (take out the trash, pick up the living room, put their toys away in the evenings, and so on), we give them a weekly allowance. When they became older, we made a list of chores along with how much money each chore was worth. This was and still is a very popular form of allowance. They do not get a set amount per week. They get paid based on what they actually do. Anyway, they must give 10 percent of the money earned to God, save 50 to 80 percent of the rest (or all if they want), and the remainder they can use for whatever they decide. We help keep their money (in envelopes) and store their savings away in a safe. We try to teach them "out of sight, out of mind"; aka less likely to spend!

Below make a list of things you do in your house to help organize chaos. You can share these with your class and hopefully come up with some great ideas to implement.

Why should we have order to our chaos? Why does it matter?

God calls us to be orderly. This is easy for some of us while others struggle, and that's okay. Complete chaos is not of God. Even with the creation of the world, God had order. Each day He created something new, and each day the new creation was dependent on the creation from the day before. He is an orderly God. He sets out a plan for each of us (Jeremiah 29:11). His plan is a process, a sequence of events that lay out our lives. Each event leads to further understanding of Him and what He has prepared for us. It is our job to teach our children order. We live in a fast-paced world. Everything we want is at our fingertips. But God calls use to slow down, remain focused on the prize (heaven), and stay the course. If we don't teach our children to follow His process, the world sure won't do it. The world will teach them the opposite.

The world's focus is on self. Everything we do should focus on making ourselves happy, successful, and accomplished. However, God created us to put the needs of others above our own. Teaching your children to help around the house is the start to putting others needs above their own. Picking up toys they didn't get out. Cleaning parts of the home, dishes, or clothes that are not their own. It's all about how you approach chores/jobs around the house.

This week I would like to challenge you to try something new in organization for your family. Now this can go one of two ways:

1. If you are an overorganizer, try to loosen up some. For example, go to bed with dirty dishes or a messy living room floor. It will be okay! I promise.

2. If you are a less organized person, implement something new to try with your family.

These are just suggestions but try something new. It may turn out to be a complete flop, or you may begin to implement this new concept occasionally. You never know until you try!

Day 2: Mapping God's Word

1 Corinthians 14:40
Write It Down and Map It Out

Define Words, Thesaurus, and Commentaries

Summary

Apply It to Your Life

Pray It Back to God

Day 3: Mapping God's Word

1 Timothy 3:4–5
Write It Down and Map It Out

Define Words, Thesaurus, and Commentaries

Summary

Apply It to Your Life

Pray It Back to God

Day 4: Mapping God's Word

Philippians 2:3
Write It Down and Map It Out

Define Words, Thesaurus, and Commentaries

Summary

Apply It to Your Life

Pray It Back to God

CHAPTER 3 REVIEW

Day 1: Order to Chaos

What types of things do you do in your home to help instill order in your chaos? Write down things you would like to share with your group this week. Remember, none of us are pros at this. Every time we implement a new idea or approach to something, it's always a trial run. Then we modify it to fit our families. What works for one family may not work for another, and that's okay.

What new process did you implement in your home this week? Was it successful? Describe what you did, how you did it, and the results. Your idea may encourage another mom to give it a try.

Day 2 through 4: Mapping God's Word

Pick one of the verses from this week to share with your class. Pick the verse that spoke the most to you. Look back over your map for this verse. Be prepared to share how you have applied or plan on applying this verse to your life.

Write this verse in the memory verse slot for chapter three in Appendix 3. Study the verse over the next several weeks. Hide His Word in your heart. Memorize.

Chapter 4

Rebekah

The babies jostled each other within her, and she said, "Why is this
happening to me?" So she went to inquire of the LORD.
—Genesis 25:22 (NIV)

Choosing Favorites

Rebekah, the wife of Isaac, was another woman from the Bible who was barren
for years. She did not have children for twenty years after marrying Isaac.
She believed she would eventually have children because of her father-in-law,
Abraham's, promise from God. He was promised that his heritage would be
many. When she did become pregnant, she had twin boys, Esau and Jacob.
We learn much about each of the boys. Esau was an outdoors guy. He loved to
go hunting and be in the wilderness. He enjoyed the wilderness so much that
he wore it around him as a coat. Jacob was quieter. He enjoyed staying back
at the tent and abide close to home. He loved to cook and prepare dishes for
the family to eat. Each son was favored by one of the parents; Isaac favored
Esau, and Rebekah favored Jacob. We learn that Jacob was closer to God than
Esau. Esau spent so much time outside, and he never learned the value of his
birthright nor his heritage from the Lord. Rebekah helped Jacob deceive Isaac
in taking Esau's birthright. Why would Rebekah do such a thing? Was she in
the wrong?

Day 1

- **Genesis 24: Abraham seeks out a wife for Isaac**
  - Verses 1–9: Abraham was too old to travel; who does he get to travel for him to seek a wife for Isaac? Where does he send him?

  - Why does he ask him to travel this distance?

  - Verses 10–14: Abraham's servant completes his journey and ask God for a sign. What does he ask?

    - How close of a relationship to God did this servant have? How can we make this assumption?

  - Verses 15–27: Rebekah appears. Who is her father? Is this important to Abraham?

    - She did as the servant had asked from God. What did the servant do in verse 21? What does this mean to you?
    - Verses 26–27: What did the servant do once he knew this woman was to be Isaac's wife?

  - Verses 28–54: Laban, Rebekah's brother, seeks out the servant and invites him to their home. The servant is treated very well and relays why he was there plus all God had done. Does Rebekah's family release her to go and marry Isaac?

- o Verses 55–61: Laban and Bethual, Rebekah's mother, did not want to let go of Rebekah right away. What was their request?

  - ▪ Were they granted their request? Why or why not?

- o Verses 62–67: What occurs when Isaac meets Rebekah?

Day 2

- **Genesis 25:20–28: Isaac marries Rebekah**
  - o Verses 20–21: How old was Isaac when he married Rebekah? _____
    - ▪ Rebekah and Isaac prayed for children. Did God provide? _____
  - o Verses 22–28: Twins are born
    - ▪ Verse 23: The babies *jostled* within her. Look up the Greek for this word:

    - ▪ Rebekah wanted to know why the babies within were so active, so she asked God. What did He tell her?

    - ▪ Verses 24–28: Describe the birth of Esau and Jacob

- Describe Esau:

- Describe Jacob:
- Rebekah loved _____; Isaac loved _____.
- **Genesis 26:6–35 Isaac lies—never a good idea!**
  - Verses 6–17
    - What did Isaac lie about?

    - Why did he lie?

    - Verse 12: God blesses Isaac in this land. Does this surprise you?

    - Verse 14: Why did the Philistines envy Isaac? What did they do out of envy?

    - This must not have stopped Isaac's success because what does the Abimelek tell Isaac in verse 16?

  - Verses 18–35: Describe the troubles Isaac faced while digging for water.

    - Verse 24–25: God brings peace to Isaac during this crazy time. What is Isaac's response to God's words?

- Verses 26–31: Abimeleck seeks out Isaac? Why? What do they create?

- Verses 34–35: How old is Esau? _____ Who does he marry? _____. Why does this cause grief to his parents?

Day 3

- **Genesis 27: Jacob tricks Isaac and runs away**
  - Verses 1–13: Describe what occurs in these thirteen verses:

  - Verses 14–17: How far does Rebekah go to deceive Isaac?

    - Why did Rebekah deceive her husband? Do some research to reach your answer.

  - Verses 18–29: Isaac blesses Jacob. Did Isaac recognize Jacob? Explain your reasoning.

  - Verses 30–41: What happens when Isaac and Esau discover the deception? Describe the situation below:

- What did Esau say he would do to Jacob?

o Verses 42–45: What is Rebekah's response to Esau's anger?

o Verses 46: Describe Rebekah's state of mind based on this verse. Explain why she was so distraught.

Day 4

- **Genesis 28: God visits Jacob**
  o Verses 1–5: Where does Isaac send Jacob, and what does he instruct him to do?

  o Verses 6–9: What does Esau do because of his father's instructions to Jacob?

  o Verses 10–22: Describe Jacob's dream and his promise from the Lord:

    - What is Jacob's response to his dream?
- Hebrews 12:16: Esau is referred to as _____.
- Romans 9:6–16: Paul refers to the lineage of Israel. Read through these scriptures, then describe why Paul was writing these words:

CHAPTER 4 REVIEW

1. Did our character this week have a relationship with God? If so, describe that relationship. Include any changes that may have occurred with this relationship.

2. Describe Rebekah's character. What can we learn from her about faith, love, marriage, being a mother, grief, strength, perseverance, and more?

3. List an example of how Rebekah handled a specific struggle. Pay attention to details. These details help teach us right steps verses wrong steps to take.

4. What can we learn about being a wife or mother from this woman's story?

Chapter 5

Merry Heart

A cheerful heart is good medicine, but a crushed spirit dries up the bones.
—Proverbs 17:22 (NIV)

Day 1: Merry Heart

Ladies, we are so blessed! Every day we should count our blessings. Our hearts should be bubbling over with gratefulness toward God for everything He has given us. Just think about that for a moment. No, I mean it! Take a moment to stop and make a list of all that God has blessed you with.

First of all, we should be overjoyed that we have the opportunity to have a relationship with Jesus Christ, our Savior. Through Jesus we have hope, something the world cannot offer us. Through Jesus we have unconditional love beyond our human minds' understanding. Through Jesus we have the gift of the Holy Spirit, which brings us love, joy, peace, patience, kindness, goodness, gentleness, and self-control. Through Jesus we have access to our Father, God. He who created us completes this trinity of compassion and never-ending love for us. This alone should build up within us a happiness and joy that the world could never give or take away. Praise Jesus!

Secondly, be thankful and joyful for your family. There are so many times we can easily focus on the struggles and downfalls in our lives, but we need to focus on the joys our families bring. Think of a time in your life (recently or over the years) when you laughed so hard that you just about peed your pants. For me, after birthing three children, I water out both ends when I laugh hard. Maybe a little too much information there—oh well. It's truth! Our families are a gift from God. In moments of frustration, disappointment, anger, or sadness, be reminded how blessed you truly are.

I find it fitting at this point to talk about family hurt. Families are messy, broken people trying to find a way to love one another without hurting one another. There are times that families fail one another. There will be times that hurtful words are spoken, inappropriate behavior is displayed, or we fail to be there for our loved ones when they need us. If you were the person that was hurt, seek God to help you find forgiveness within your heart. If you were the person that caused the hurt, seek God to help you find the words to ask for forgiveness. True forgiveness comes through Christ. In either situation, Christ needs to be at the center of any conversation that occurs. Be reminded of Romans 3:23: "For all have sinned and fall short of the glory of God." The process of true, complete forgiveness takes time, and it is a process. If you are struggling to forgive or to ask for forgiveness, seek help through a Christian mentor, pastor, or counselor.

Thirdly, be thankful for the joy from all the other aspects of your life: true friendships, your job, your schooling, your pets, your neighbors, your church family, and whatever else you can think of. God puts us right where He wants us, right where we need to be.

One of the best things we can do for our children is to be joyful. This world can quickly remind us of sorrow and pain. If we allow it, our circumstances can take over our joy. We must constantly remind ourselves of our heavenly Father's plan for our lives. He wants us to prosper. He sets good things before us, but sometimes we do not recognize them. We must search within each circumstance to find the joy of Jesus inside. If not for ourselves, we must dig deep for our children. I spent several years of my life as a sad, young momma. I was overwhelmed by Satan's lies and tricks. He had me convinced that I would never be the mother I should be to my children. He told me I was not even worthy of being a mother. Every mistake I made in life, Satan magnified it in my mind. Don't allow Satan to steal your joy. Your joy comes from above. Satan has no power unless we choose to give him the power. I stand with you today in agreement that Satan can take a hike from your thoughts. Open your eyes fully so you can see God in all your circumstances. Sometimes you have to fight the darkness every day, but I know you can make it through. I found my joy in Jesus. To this day, I wake up each morning asking my Father to fill me with the joy of the Holy Spirit. When days are tough and the world is suffocating me, I remind myself that I am a child of the one true king. The world has no power over me. Believe it, ladies! Stand on it! Trust it!

Okay, let's get down to business. Let's celebrate our lives!

- Take some time to journal, pray, or illustrate your happiness that Jesus is in your life. I can't imagine life without Him. He is our Savior, Redeemer, risen Lord, master, Emmanuel, alpha and omega, advocate, deliverer, the I Am, lamb of God, mediator, Messiah, the way. Who is Jesus to you today?

- Take a moment to thank God for all the provisions He has blessed you with: your husband and your job (even you stay-at-home moms!). You've got a hard job. Has God blessed you financially in ways that make no sense to this world? Include those as you journal thanks to God.

- Can you think of a funny family memory? Something that caused you to laugh so hard you were shedding water at both ends? Write a summary of this experience below. Be ready to share about this experience with your group this week.

Day 2: Mapping God's Word

Proverbs 12:25
Write It Down and Map It Out

Define Words, Thesaurus, and Commentaries

Summary

Apply It to Your Life

Pray It Back to God

Day 3: Mapping God's Word

Psalm 126:2
Write It Down and Map It Out

Define Words, Thesaurus, and Commentaries

Summary

Apply It to Your Life

Pray It Back to God

Day 4: Mapping God's Word

Proverbs 15:15
Write It Down and Map It Out

Define Words, Thesaurus, and Commentaries

Summary

Apply It to Your Life

Pray It Back to God

CHAPTER 5 REVIEW

Day 1: Merry Heart

Go back to your journaling this week. Select sections that you would like to share with your group this week. Laughter is good medicine. Find something to share that will bring joy and laughter to your class. Or you can write a new memory below to share. These are the memories we will pass down from generation to generation. Experiences that bring us joy should be treasured inside of our hearts. Place them inside your heart, so you can quickly be reminded of times of joy when trouble surrounds you.

Day 2 through 4: Mapping God's Word

Pick one of the verses from this week to share with your class. Pick the verse that spoke the most to you. Look back over your map for this verse. Be prepared to share how you have applied or plan on applying this verse to your life.

Write this verse in the memory verse slot for chapter five in Appendix 3. Study the verse over the next several weeks. Hide His Word in your heart. Memorize.

Chapter 6

Elizabeth

But the angel of the Lord said to him: "Do not be afraid,
Zachariah; your prayer has been heard. Your wife Elizabeth
will bear you a son, and you are to call him John.
—Luke 1:13 (NIV)

A Worshipper of God

Elizabeth (also spelled Elisabeth) was the wife of a priest named Zachariah (also spelled Zacharias). She became the mother of John the Baptist, the forerunner of Jesus Christ. What an honor! God did not place this honor on just anyone. He chose Elizabeth for a reason. As we learn about her life, we find many attributes of a God-fearing woman.

Day 1

- **Luke 1:1–4**
  - Luke, known as a companion of Paul, began his writings by emphasizing that his writings were truth based on his own research and testimonies of others who had witnessed Jesus.
    - We know that the first four chapters of the New Testament are referred to as the Gospels. Do you know who wrote them? Or what order they were written in? Do some digging to find out.

- **Luke 1:5–9**
  - Verse 5:
    - Luke references the king of Judea, Herod. Herod was one of the decedents of Esau (we discussed when we studied Rebekah). Herod was a very cruel and terrible king. He executed many people, including members of his own family. This sets the scene for Elizabeth's times.
    - We are introduced to Zachariah—a priest from the division of Abijah. (If you would like further history about this priest division, read 1 Chronicles 23–24.)
    - We are introduced to Zachariah's wife, Elizabeth, the daughter of Aaron. What does this tell you about her lineage?

  - Verses 6–7: Both Zachariah and Elizabeth were righteous before God walking blameless, but above all that, what was their struggle?

  - Verses 8–9: Research to find out what Luke meant by "his lot fell to burn incense when he went to the temple of the Lord."

Day 2

- **Luke 1:10–20**
  - Verse 10: Who was with Zachariah in the temple? How do you know?

  - Verse 11: Who appeared before Zachariah? _____. Where was he standing?

o   Verse 12: What was Zachariah's reaction?

o   Verses 13–17: What was the message Zachariah received? What specific instructions were given to him regarding the baby?

o   Verse 18: Did Zachariah believe the angel? _____ Why or why not?

o   Verse 19: How did the angel respond to Zachariah's disbelief? Do you sense a hint of authority in his words?

o   Verse 20: What was Zachariah's punishment? Do you find any significance in this punishment for his sin?

Day 3

- **Luke 1:21–25**
    o   Verse 21–23: What occurred when Zachariah came out of the temple?

    o   Verse 24: Once pregnant, Elizabeth remained in seclusion for five months. Why?

    o   Verse 25: Why was Elizabeth so happy to be pregnant?

- **Luke 1:26–38: Story of Mary and Gabriel**
  - o How is this story representative Elizabeth's story?

- **Luke 1:39–41**
  - o Describe Mary and Elizabeth's greeting.

  - o Verse 41: This verse tells us that Elizabeth was filled with the Holy Spirit. How could this be? Jesus had not even been to earth yet. Can you explain this?

- **Luke 1:42–45**
  - o Describe Elizabeth's exclamation.

Day 4

- **Luke 1:46–55**
  - o Describe Mary's prayer.

- **Luke 1:56–57**
  - o How long did Mary stay with Elizabeth?

- **Luke 1:58**
  - o How does this verse relate to verse 35?

- **Luke 1:59–66: John's circumcision**
  - What did the people want to name the baby? How did Elizabeth and Zachariah deal with this?

  - What happened to Zachariah's voice?

  - How did the people react to this?

- **Luke 1:67–79**
  - Verse 67: Zachariah was also filled with the Holy Spirit! How amazing is that?

  - Describe Zachariah's prophesy.

- **Luke 1:80**
  - John grew and became strong in _____, and he lived in the _____ until he appeared publicly in _____.

CHAPTER 6 REVIEW

1. Did our character this week have a relationship with God? If so, describe that relationship. Include any changes that may have occurred with this relationship.

2. Describe Elizabeth's character. What can we learn from her about faith, love, marriage, being a mother, grief, strength, perseverance, and more?

3. List an example of how Elizabeth handled a specific struggle. Pay attention to details. These details help teach us the right steps versus the wrong steps to take.

4. What can we learn about being a wife or mother from this woman's story?

Chapter 7
Sacrificial Love

Greater love has no one than this; to lay down one's life for one's friends.
—John 15:13 (NIV)

Day 1: Sacrificial Love

No man can express the same sacrificial love for us as Christ demonstrated on the cross. The pain and agony He endured was excruciating. I can't even imagine how He felt; betrayed by those who loved Him, tortured before His own people, beaten until He no longer looked human, and then forced to carry His own cross to the place where He was to be crucified. When I watched the movie *Passion of the Christ* by Mel Gibson, I was beyond mortified and brought to tears. My Savior, Jesus, did this for me. Everything He endured was to bring me peace and hope.

Throughout the Bible, there are four different types of love described. These are the Greek words and meanings:

- Eros: sensual or romantic love[v]
- Storge: family love or an affectionate bond[vi]
- Philia: powerful emotional bond seen in deep friendships[vii]
- Agape: God's love in action; the love Jesus displayed on the cross [viii]

When reading scripture, it is important to find the context of the word *love*. This helps us to determine what type of love God is referring to. As you continue this week, keep these four different Greek words in mind.

Okay, moms, there are no words that can describe the birth of your child (or the official adoption of your child). I can still remember each of my children's births. When I look past all the pain, I see such an anxious anticipation to finally see my child's face, to touch his or her little fingers, and to hear that first cry. God gives us nine months to prepare our hearts to be mothers. If you have gone through the process of adoption, you may not have even had that much time. Or you may have had much longer. If you struggled to become pregnant, you are beyond ready to experience motherhood. Many women experience the pain of miscarriage and struggle with a different type of anticipation of motherhood. Either way, your anticipation helped build this love for your child—a love that has no boundaries, a love that sees to the heart, a love that drives you to become better at life, a love that sometimes clouds our judgment, and a love like *agape* love.

Children are our lives. We get to experience firsts with our children. We get upset if we miss their first word, the first time they roll over, their first steps, and more. We want experience everything with them. We don't want to miss out on anything. Taking part in these firsts allows us to show our love as excitement in overcoming boundaries and obstacles as they grow and develop.

As they grow, we must turn our love into discipline. We love them enough to teach them right from wrong. We set boundaries for our children because we love them. Keeping them in these boundaries is a daily struggle. It pulls at us emotionally, physically, and spiritually. We become emotionally exhausted as we continue to discipline our children for the same thing over and over again. We also emotionally struggle, wondering if we are too hard or too easy on them at times. We physically become exhausted after keeping our word and following through on discipline. Many times our choices for discipline hurt us more than our children. We don't like to see them sad or become emotional because of discipline. Spiritually, Satan knows we love our children and don't want to see them hurting, so he uses that against us when we follow through with discipline. If he can keep us from disciplining our children, he has a better chance at tempting them. Discipline teaches respect, love, and expectations. All things that Satan hates to see.

By the way, every child is different. Therefore, discipline looks different for each child. And that's okay! In our house, we used various methods to teach our children right from wrong. When my children were young, a close Christian mentor told me that the punishment should fit the crime. We have tried to use that thought process when deciding how to discipline in our home. If our children slammed their doors, they lost them for a week. If they talked back to us, we put a drop of soap on their tongue (except for my son Caleb—he liked the soap). If they disobeyed us by wasting our time, we used a time-out. It was a constant battle every day to stick to our word, follow through with discipline, and then always follow up each episode by talking out the situation with them.

We always took the time to talk it out after the child faced the punishment. This is critical. These talks help children understand why they were punished. Communication is key in all relationships in life. Don't forget to apply it with your children. After talking to our children, we would have them repeat to us why they were punished. We wanted to make sure they knew why. We would also use scripture to help our children see why their choice was not a good one. This helps immensely when dealing with small to major issues. Always use God's Word with discipline. It helps keep your focus in the right place. Plus this shows our children that God is our rock and foundation.

I think it is fitting here to say that no child should ever be punished by a beating that leaves welts or bruises. There are too many people that take discipline too far. If you struggle with stopping yourself and find that you have hurt your child, seek professional help. Satan will try to convince you to be ashamed of your actions. Don't listen to him. Seek out someone to talk to, someone you can trust who will help you find a method to control your anger. This happens more than we would like to admit. Don't give in to Satan's lies when he tries to convince you that you were never meant to be a mother. God is the giver of life. He blessed you with children because He knew you could be a good mom. Find your strength and hope in Him.

I also would like to point out that everyone disciplines differently, and that's okay too. Only give advice to others if they ask for it. At times we can become very adamant that our way is the best method. It may work for your children but not necessarily for other children. Yes, God calls us to discipline. But don't become too pushy on what's the right and wrong way to handle it. There are extremes in both directions: way too easy and way too hard. If you feel very strongly about approaching someone, seek God first. He will direct you on what to do. Never approach someone without seeking God, unless a child is in immediate danger.

That being said, how do you feel about yourself in this area? Do you struggle with following through? Do you send out false warnings to your children, but when it comes down to it, you give them another chance? This is not something you will have to discuss with your group this week. Be honest with yourself and with God. He already knows anyway. Write a prayer to God below about the subject of discipline.

Day 2: Sacrificial Love

How does agape love and discipline go together? God's love for us is immeasurable and incomparable. He would do anything for you. History testifies to this. With this love, He also disciplines us. Scripture is very clear that we are held to a standard. We have been given the Ten Commandments to follow. Throughout scripture we read stories of people who were disciplined by God: punishment came when they did not follow God's ways. Many of the women that we study using *Moms like Christ* give us a glimpse into their lives, and we see God disciplining them. Why would God discipline those He loves?

Read 1 Corinthians 13:4-8 below:

> Love is patient, love is kind. It does not envy, it does not boast, it is
> not proud. It does not dishonor others, it is not self-seeking, it is not

easily angered, it keeps no record of wrongs. Love does not delight in evil but rejoices with the truth. It always protects, always trust, always hopes, always perseveres. Love never fails.

Wow, that's our description of agape love, such high standards. It almost seems impossible in the world we live in. But it is possible! God gave us these instructions to help keep us on the straight and narrow way. How will our children develop agape love if we don't show them? To teach patience, we must first be impatient. To teach kindness, we must first be unkind. To teach humbleness, we must first be boastful, proud, or envious. To teach honor, we must dishonor. To teach respect for others above ourselves, we must first be selfish. To teach self-control, we must be angry or frustrated. To teach forgiveness, we must be unforgiving. To teach what is right, we must know what is wrong. To teach what is truth, we must know what is false.

Love is something that we learn through life lessons. Many of these things can be taught to young children but don't truly take root until they are older and more mature. So when you make a rule and it is broken, do not hesitate to follow through with discipline. Teach your children the ways of the Lord. Start young, and as they mature, it will become easier. There are the terrible twos and the horrible thirteens. Just remember to never back down. Our children depend on us to teach them. They must learn it from us because the world has lessons too—lessons that teach the opposite of God's Word.

There are many scriptures that are useful as your rock for disciplining. We will be studying two of them this week in our mapping God's Word sections. With your husband, seek scriptures to stand on throughout the many seasons of life with your family. Different seasons may call for difference scriptures. Be ready with an answer. Be willing to be the disciplinarian and know that it's okay.

Day 3: Mapping God's Word

Hebrews 12:11
Write It Down and Map It Out

Define Words, Thesaurus, and Commentaries

Summary

Apply It to Your Life

Pray It Back to God

Day 4: Mapping God's Word

Proverbs 3:11–12
Write It Down and Map It Out

Define Words, Thesaurus, and Commentaries

Summary

Apply It to Your Life

Pray It Back to God

CHAPTER 7 REVIEW

Day 1–2: Sacrificial Love

Write a prayer to God for giving us agape love. Ask Him to guide you as a parent, working alongside your husband to set boundaries for your children. God knows your children even better than you do. Seek advice from Him. This prayer does not have to be shared with your group unless you find healing from sharing it.

Have you been hurt by discipline in your life? It is okay to be open and honest about it. These things happen. As a child, I experienced harsh discipline that did not lead me toward agape love. Instead of using discipline to teach me about God, it was used to control me. I dealt with anger, lying, deception, and more. It was very hard for me until I was introduced to agape love related to discipline. I always saw discipline as an abuse mechanism. But God set it up as a love mechanism. Teaching sacrificial love through discipline is a much better approach. But if you have been hurt in the past, you may find it difficult to do. Do not feel obligated currently to share your story. It is part of your testimony. Our testimonies are meant to be shared, to help equip others going through the same things we experienced. Consider writing down your testimony. I have done this. It brought me healing, guidance, and above all else, I became closer to God.

What methods of discipline has your family found productive? Your idea may spark something in someone else.

Day 3 and 4: Mapping God's Word

Pick one of the verses from this week to share with your class. Pick the verse that spoke the most to you. Look back over your map for this verse. Be prepared to share how you have applied or plan on applying this verse to your life.

Write this verse in the memory verse slot for chapter seven in Appendix 3. Study the verse over the next several weeks. Hide His Word in your heart. Memorize.

*You may have another verse that your family stands on for discipline. Feel free to share that verse with your group this week.

Chapter 8

Mary, Mother of Jesus

They all joined together constantly in prayer, along with the women
and Mary the mother of Jesus, and with his brothers.
—Acts 1:14 (NIV)

How Do You Raise Jesus as Your Son?

Mary, mother of Jesus, was an amazing woman of God; a humble village woman from Nazareth chosen by God to be Jesus's earthly mother. Wow, what an honor. She must have walked upright, for she found favor in God's eyes. I can't wait to get to heaven and talk to Mary. I'm sure she will be holding women's conferences twenty-four hours every day. Many people on earth see her as a saint; someone who is to be praised and worshipped. I do admire her for being selected by God, but she is no higher than any other human on earth. However, we can learn from her life. We can strive to be like her.

We will look at Mary's story from all three Gospels. We will search for parallels and find new insights we can learn from each writing.

Day 1

- **Luke 1:26–38: Mary has a visitor**
  - ○ Verses 26–27
    - ▪ How far along was Elizabeth with John the Baptist when Mary has her visit with the angel? _____

- Where did Mary live? _____
  - Do some research about this town in these days. Was it a booming city?

- Joseph was a descendant of whom? _____
- Point: These verses confirm that Mary was a virgin.
  o Verses 28–29
    - Verse 28: What does the angel mean by "highly favored, the Lord is with you"?
    - Verse 29: Did Mary understand the angel's greeting? _____. Explain how you know.

  - Study verses 30–33. What was the angel telling Mary? Where in the Old Testament were these things foretold?

  - Verses 34–37: Mary questions how this will be possible. What is the angel's reply?
  - Verse 38: What is Mary's response to the angel's words? What does this tell us about Mary?
- **Luke 1:39–45: Elizabeth confirms the angel's words**
  o Who did Mary go to visit with her news? _____. Do you find it interesting that in a time of uncertainty she reaches out to a close friend? Someone she can trust with anything? I like that.
  o Verses 41–45 How does the Holy Spirit work through Elisabeth to confirm Mary's story from the angel?
- **Matthew 1:18–25: Joseph, it's okay**
  o Verses 18: So Mary is pledged to marry _____, but before they came together, she was found _____ by the _____ _____.

o Verses 19–25: What happens to Joseph that confirms her immaculate conception?

o Do some research to discover a few things with these verses:
   ▪ Did Mary tell Joseph about the baby? Or did Joseph find out from the angel?

   ▪ How far along was Mary when Joseph found out about the baby?

Day 2

- **Luke 2:1–5: Going on a trip**
  o Why did Joseph and Mary have to travel to Bethlehem?

- **Luke 2:6–7: Jesus is born**
  o Where was Jesus born? Do you see any parallels between a humble village girl from Nazareth and the place of His birth? What is God trying to show us here?

- **Luke 2:8–20: Visitors**
  o Make a list of words the angel uses to describe Jesus.
  o The shepherds go visit Jesus. Where was the baby when they got to the stable? _____ Do you think there is any significance to this?
  o Once the visit was over, the shepherds left and spread the word about the baby.

    o   Verse 19: What did Mary do once they left?

        ▪   Why do you think God put this verse in the Bible?

- **Luke 2:21–39: A trip to Jerusalem**
  o   Even though it had been prophesied that Jesus would be sinless, Joseph and Mary still followed Jewish customs. On the eighth day, they left to head toward Jerusalem for His circumcision. They had no idea what amazing things were about to take place.
  o   Verses 21–24: What all did Joseph and Mary must do for Jesus in Jerusalem?

Day 3

    o   Verses 25–35: Simeon
        ▪   Who was Simeon?

        ▪   What did he do when he saw Jesus?

        ▪   Verse 33: These scriptures say Joseph and Mary marveled at what was said about Jesus. Why do you think this happened? They knew who He was already.

        ▪   Verses 34–35: Simeon's words to Mary are bittersweet. What was Simeon referring too?

- **Luke 2:36–38**
  - o Describe Anna. Who was she and what did she do?

- **Luke 2:39–40**
  - o Where was Jesus's hometown? _____
  - o Verse 40: Jesus grew and became _____; He was filled with _____; and the _____ if God was upon Him.
- **Matthew 2:11–23: The Magi visit**
  - o Verses 11–12: The Magi see Jesus and Mary, and they worship Jesus and give Him their gifts. Even though Herod asked them to let him know where the King was, they don't return to Herod. Why?

  - o Verse 13–15: Describe what occurs in these verses.

  - o Verses 16–23: All of these verses confirm that Jesus is the Messiah. Why?

- **Luke 2:41–52: Festival of the Passover**
  - o How old was Jesus in this story? _____
  - o Parent fail 1: Joseph and Mary left Jesus in Jerusalem. Oops! How far did they travel? _____Jesus was old enough to know right from wrong. As parents, Joseph and Mary must have given Jesus some leeway about traveling. He had earned their trust.
  - o How many days did they search for Jesus? _____ Where did they find Him? What was He doing there?

o What was Mary's reaction? How would you have reacted?

o What was Jesus's reaction to His mother?

o Verse 50: What had happened to Joseph and Mary? Hadn't they known from the beginning that Jesus was God's Son? Why do you think they were confused here?

o Verse 51: Jesus went back home with them. Again, we see the words "his mother treasured all these things in her heart." What does this mean to you?

o Verse 52: Jesus continued to grow in wisdom, stature, and in favor with _____ and _____.

Day 4

- **John 2:1–11**
  o Verses 1–2: They were attending a wedding in _____. Who was there?

  o Verses 3–5: Uh oh, no more wine. What does Mary do? Why do you think she did this?
  o Verses 4–11: Describe Jesus's first miracle.

- Do you find it interesting that even though He said, "My hour has not yet come," He still obeyed His mother?

- Verse 11: How did the miracle affect His disciples?

- **John 2:12**
  o Who traveled with Jesus after the wedding? He brought His mother. Do you find this surprising?

  o Is there evidence in the Bible that Mary traveled with Jesus other times?
- **John 19:25–27: Jesus on the cross**
  o Describe how you think Mary felt in this verse.

  o Even as He was dying, Jesus thought of His mother. What does this tell you about Jesus's relationship with His mother?
- **Acts 1:14: Mary is still going about her Son's business**
  o Mary joined her son and the disciples to do what?
  o What does this tell you about Mary as Jesus's mother?

CHAPTER 8 REVIEW

1. Did our character this week have a relationship with God? If so, describe that relationship. Include any changes that may have occurred with this relationship.

2. Describe Mary's character. What can we learn from her about faith, love, marriage, being a mother, grief, strength, perseverance, and more?

3. List an example of how Mary handled a specific struggle. Pay attention to details. These details help teach us right steps verses wrong steps to take.

4. What can we learn about being a wife or mother from this woman's story?

Appendix 1

Example of Mapping God's Word

Ephesians 6:18
Write It Down and Map It Out

"And pray in the Spirit on all occasions with all kinds of prayers and requests. With this in mind, be alert and always keep on praying for all the Lord's people."

Define Words, Thesaurus, and Commentaries

"Be alert" = agrypneo (Greek) be sleepless, keep awake, watch[ix]

David Guzik:

"all kinds of prayers" = group prayers, individual prayers, silent prayer, shouting prayer, walking prayer, kneeling prayer, eloquent prayer, groaning prayer, constant prayer, fervent prayer—just pray.

We can battle spiritually not only on our own behalf, but also on behalf of others. [x]

Summary

In all circumstances pray, even when I'm not sure how or what to say. Pray for all those around me as well. Pray with those around me. Never stop praying. Prayer not just limited to speaking audibly while knelt on the floor. Prayer can be done in silence or by speaking. I can pray alone, with another person, or with several people. My prayers should never cease. My thoughts, my words, and my actions should always reflect a prayerful spirit. My prayer life should not just revolve around my needs or desires. I am commanded to go before the Lord for my brothers and sisters in Christ.

Apply It to Your Life

No matter what I am facing—joy, tribulation, happiness, inability to forgive, anger, sorrow —go to God and pray. Prayer is one of my major communication tools with Him. If I lack talking to God, it's my fault. I need to prioritize my life to make sure prayer is a part of it. Not just a part of my daily routine, but a daily need. My desire to communicate with God through prayer should be on the forefront of my mind. Pray when I wake and when I lie down. Pray when I am alone and when I am among others. Pray when I see a need of my own or another person's. In all situations, pray.

Pray It Back to God

God, forgive me for lacking in my communication with You. I love You. I admire all I see You do in my life and in the lives of those around me. You are my one desire. I need You in my life. I can't make it through without You. I long to tell You about my day, my life, my hurts, my joys, and to share with You all I encounter. Help me to more alert for those in need. I want others to see You in me. I want others to find the peace I find in You. Help me to take moments to pray with others. I want to be more like You. Thank You for Your leadership. Thank You for Your love. Thank You for meeting me right where I am every time I need You. You are my Savior, and I adore You!

Appendix 2

Memorization Techniques

Beginning in chapter 1, I encourage each woman to select a verse to memorize. She may choose from the weekly focus verses or select one of her own. These verses are used as building blocks for implementing a closer walk with the Lord. He is our rock that we build our foundation upon. There is never going to be a better time than the present to add to our foundation.

Your job is to encourage each woman to select a verse that she can apply to her life now and into the future. One she can stand on as she continues her daily walk in this battlefield of life. If anyone is struggling to select verses, come prepared with your own verses to share; verses that have helped you stand when the world would rather see you fall.

Here is a list of suggestions you may use to help these women conquer the struggle of memorization. These are methods I have used through the years. One method may work well for one person, while another person needs to try another method. Allow women to figure out which method works the best for them.

- Write out your verse on an index card. Read the card over and over—not just in your head but say the words out loud. The next day hand the card to another person. Recite the verse from memory.
  - Highlight, underline, or circle key words. When memorizing, refer to these key words to help you remember the entire verse.

o Put the reference for the verse on both sides of the card. That way if you need to study alone, you can always look at the side with the reference and then recite the verse.

■ You may find that putting the key words on the side with the reference will also help you memorize the verse.

- The more you write, read, and hear the verse, the easier it will be to memorize it.

o Write the verse over and over in your journal or just on scrap paper. This may seem silly, but you may find this is just what gets you through.

- Use a different translation: be careful that you don't lose the true meaning of the verse by watering it down.

- Make flash cards to play memory as you add more and more verses to your list.

- Keep all your verses on together: use a key ring, spiral notebook, or any other organization method.

Appendix 3

Memory Verses

Chapter 1: Massive Prayer Life
Chapter 3: Order to Chaos
Chapter 5: Merry Heart
Chapter 7: Sacrificial Love

Appendix 4

Teacher Leader Guide

First of all, thank you! Stepping up and leading a women's Bible study is not an easy task. I appreciate your time and effort (emotionally, mentally, physically, and spiritually). God will bless you for your efforts. No doubt in my mind!

How long do I need to set up my weekly meetings?

How many women should be in my group?

- ✓ 5–7 women = 1-hour class time (on average). We all know how a group of women can talk, talk, talk …
- ✓ 8–10 women = 1½-hour class time
- ✓ 10 or more = 2-hour class time

How long is this class designed to take?

- Week 1 is an introduction to the book series. Read through the introduction, it's about a Relationship, Make a Commitment, and Mapping God's Word.
- Each additional week should cover one chapter in the book (weeks 2–9). Spend the week reading the chapter. Discuss the end-of-chapter review at your next meeting.
- Optional week (10) to just get together to celebrate all you have gained through this study.

Basics of Leading a Women's Bible Study

Use these steps to prepare yourself to lead this group of women:

1. **Be prepared for anything**. While writing this book, God has shown me there will be women who go through this Bible study who are experiencing struggles. Please be respectful of their privacy.

    a. **Do not force women to share if they do not feel comfortable sharing**. This will only increase their anxiety and disappointment in themselves.

    b. **Be respectful of time**. Women are giving their time to meet with you. Please keep the classes moving along. Now, don't move so fast that women feel they cannot share their hearts. If a lesson takes two weeks instead of one, so be it. As long as the extra time is useful. Useful means uplifting women and drawing them closer to Jesus. Use your discernment. God will let you know when to push on and when to just sit and listen.

       i. If you find a woman in your class is taking up a lot of time that takes away from other women being able to share, talk to her one-on-one. Sometimes these women just need someone to listen. Be that ear and express your concern, in love, to them.

       ii. If at any time conflict arises between any women (including yourself or any participants), sit down with the women involved and talk through the struggle. Seek assistance from an elder's wife or pastor in extreme situations when you need help to make peace.

2. **Lead by example**. Each week have your lessons finished to the best of your ability, memorize your verses, share your testimony (seasons of your life that apply to the lessons in the book), and whatever God leads you to share.

3. **Be an encourager to all women**. You will have women from all walks of life, all levels of spirituality, and all emotional status. Don't expect everyone to be the same. Only speak to uplift and never tell a woman she is doing it wrong. Maybe you can make suggestions, but don't be too pushy. We want the women in your Bible study to feel comfortable with their surroundings. It's God's job to make us feel uncomfortable when we are not reaching up to His potential for our lives. Let the Holy Spirit weed out those that need motivating. God works in mysterious ways. Don't get in His way. Let Him lead.

4. **Bring snacks**. We women—well, probably men too and children—love to eat! You can make it healthy or not. Coffee, hot cocoa, or tea are great too.

Procedures to follow when leading this book

First meeting with your group:

1. "Get to know you" activity
    a. Find an activity that will fit the group of ladies you will be meeting with. Share names, number of kids, hobbies, funny stories, whatever works. This will help break the ice to get your group talking together.
2. Read through the introduction of this book and the It's about a Relationship section.
    a. Emphasize the importance of keeping everything discussed together private. Otherwise, you will not gain as much as you could with these women.
    b. Let the women know that if there are struggles, they need to come and talk to you about them.
    c. A relationship with Jesus Christ is by far the most important part of this journey.
3. Read and sign the Make a Commitment pledge
4. Go through the Mapping God's Word example briefly. Encourage your group to refer back to this section for their weekly quiet times.
5. Explain weekly procedures:
    a. Each week is set up by five days per chapter: Days 1, 2, 3, and 4 plus the review day.
        i. All materials on these pages need to be completed before the following meeting time.
        ii. The review page at the end of each week will be used for discussion at your weekly meetings.

Weekly meetings:

1. Weeks 1, 3, 5, and 7:
    i. Review chosen memory verses. Partner up and practice reciting memory verses. Each week recite all the memory verses you have from previous *Moms Like Christ* studies plus this book.

ii. Discuss the review questions as a class. Allow women to share their responses, but do not force anyone to speak.

iii. Each woman should share one verse she mapped this week. (This is the part that will take the majority of your class time).

    1. Share each section of their verse map.

2. Weeks 2, 4, 6, and 8:

    i. Review memory verses from previous weeks. The more repetition, the longer you will remember the verses.

    ii. Discuss the four questions from that week's Bible character study day 5 review page.

        1. Allow women to express their findings, even if they are different from your own. You may find something new that someone else discovered.

        2. I have included summaries of each Bible character in this book. These summaries may have information you wish to share with your group. Use them as you see fit.

Let's keep in contact

I would love for you to contact me and let me know how things are going. I would love to chat or answer any questions you may have. I can share your stories on the book's Facebook page. I want to support you in any I can. I definitely want to pray for you. So seek me out!

My contact information:

Email: csbibler@mail.com

Facebook page: Moms Like Christ by Sarah L. Bibler

*This is a public page. You are more than welcome to follow me and post pictures or comments about the progress of your class. Do not post any personal information of any woman in your group. You can invite them to my page, and they can post any personal information for themselves. I would love to see pictures of your group of ladies! That will help me when I'm praying for your class. I can put faces to the groups out there.

Appendix 5

Women of the Bible

I have included summaries about each woman studied in this book. You may use these summaries as a reference to review before each week. You are free to share these with your group if you find it useful. Use them as you see fit.

Chapter 2

Eunice

Eunice, Timothy's mother, is noted for having an amazing legacy of faith. Scriptures confirm that her mother, Lois, shared Old Testament scriptures with her. These stories she then passed down to her own children. It is noted in scripture that she married a Gentile. I find this so interesting since she was raised by a mother known to teach and stand for God's ways. We have no idea if he shared her love for God or not. Timothy must have grown very close to his mother and grandmother. He must have heard their stories over and over again. During his mentoring time with Paul, on several occasions Paul calls Timothy to be reminded of the stories he was told by his mother and grandmother. Oh, to be noted so highly by Paul, a man of God.

To truly understand Eunice's legacy, we must study Timothy. His success as an evangelist is partly due to his mother. Try to grasp the whole picture here: Timothy, a young man possibly in his twenties, taken under Paul's wing, leads to the understanding of who Jesus was and is, mentored by Paul to take on his legacy of evangelism, persecuted alongside Paul, and watches Paul's execution. And still he stays on the path of preaching the Word. This is a man who any mother would proudly call her son.

Makes me wonder what type of legacy am I leaving for my children? Grandchildren?

What can we learn from Eunice:

1. Eunice was attentive and listened to her mother's stories about God.
2. Eunice believed her mother and shared her faithful stories with her children. Because of her faithfulness, her son shared her love for God and became an evangelist.

> "I am reminded of your sincere faith, a faith that dwelt first in your grandmother Lois and your mother Eunice and now, I am sure, dwells in your as well." 2 Timothy 1:5 (ESV)

Quick question: In your opinion, would Timothy have been such an inspirational apostle for God if his mother (and grandmother) had not passed down the sacred stories? How important is it that we share sacred stories with our children and grandchildren?

Chapter 4

Rebekah

God has His hand in putting Rebekah and Isaac together. Her servant's heart is what set her up to be Isaac's wife. Now, this being an arranged marriage, who would expect for the couple to fall madly in love with each other? But Isaac loved Rebekah and she loved him. God was so good to Isaac. When his mom died, he was very upset. Rebekah brought back happiness in his life.

She was barren. Isaac prayed to the Lord for they longed to bear a child. When she became pregnant, she felt the babies fighting within her. She asked the Lord what was going on. He told her the children would fight against each other. In fact, the older one would serve the younger. That was not the way things normally worked out in these times. The older child should be the bearer of the father's blessing. But it seemed that God had something else in mind for these children. For nine months she carried these boys. I wonder if they fought often. As a mother, this would have troubled me. Wondering why God would create two young men that would be so against each other. This would have been nine months of many trials—emotionally and mentally.

When Esau was born, he was completely red and hairy; doesn't sound too appealing to me. He became obsessed with nature. He loved to be out in the wilderness, hunting or scavenging around. He was definitely the wilder child of the two. Isaac seemed to love Esau more. The scriptures say it was because Isaac loved venison. Esau was the one to hunt the venison. However, Jacob was the cook of the family. He made it taste good.

Jacob was born holding on to Esau's foot—interesting! Jacob was a plain man. He preferred to just hang out in their home. Rebekah loved Jacob. She saw something in him that Esau did not have.

The first trouble we read about after birth is when Jacob stole Esau's birthright. I wonder why Esau so easily gave it up. In these times, the birthright was a valuable attribute to possesses. It included material and spiritual dynamics. The son with the birthright received a double portion of the inheritance and also became the head of the family and the spiritual leader after the father was gone. In this specific case, the birthright would include the covenant between God and Abraham of land, a nation, and a messiah. Esau saw no value in the birthright. This makes me wonder how close of a relationship he had with God. Jacob had already been promised the birthright before he was even born (God's promise to Rebekah). But he still went through the actions of stealing it from Esau.

Esau grieved his parents later in life when he took a wife from a tribe not associated with his family's line. God had told Abraham that his offspring were not to marry women of Canaan, but Esau disobeyed this direct order from God. This grieved his parents greatly. I'm sure they shared stories with Esau about God's promises to their family, but I also wonder if Esau knew the promise about his brother, Jacob. God had said before he was born that he would serve his brother, Jacob. He had already given his birthright to Jacob. It seems like Esau had a rebellious spirit within him.

When Isaac became old, he told Esau that he wanted to give him his birthright. Isaac knew God had told Rebekah the birthright should go to Jacob. But Isaac wasn't thinking with his spiritual mind, he was thinking with his human mind. He loved Esau more and appreciated his hunting and venison. Of course, Rebekah overheard Isaac's conversation with Esau, and she decided to help Jacob deceive Isaac rather than just wait on God. God always keeps His promises. But just like Isaac, Rebekah used her human thoughts rather than her spiritual mind. Both Isaac and Rebekah thought they had control of the birthright. However, God had it all set in stone since the beginning.

In the end, Esau threatens to kill Jacob. Jacob must flee. And the family is divided. All because they decided to try to fix things for themselves instead of allowing God's plan to unravel on its own. Wow—sound familiar? Not the murder part but doing things on our own without thought to what God says.

What we can learn from Rebekah:

1. Rebekah had a servant's heart when she first became Isaac's wife. God had equipped her with this gift.

> "She said, 'Drink my lord.' And she quickly let down her jar
> upon her hand, and gave him drink." (Genesis 24:18)

2. Rebekah knew God, because she recognized His voice when He spoke to her.

> "And the LORD said unto her, 'Two nations are in your womb, and
> two people from within you shall be divided; the one shall be stronger
> than the other, the older shall serve the younger.'" (Genesis 25:23)

3. Rebekah took matters into her own hands instead of waiting on God's timing. This caused family strife and division.

> "Now therefore, my son, obey my voice as I command you." (Genesis 27:8)

Chapter 6

Elizabeth

Elizabeth means 'God is my oath," which means "worshipper of God." According to Luke, Elizabeth was "one of the daughters of Aaron," which means she came of an honored priestly line (Exodus 6:23). Her husband was also a priest. John had priestly decedents on both sides. She grew up knowing firsthand what offerings and rituals the Israelites followed. She was one of the first people who had the presence of the Holy Spirit even before the birth of Christ. She had a close relationship (family and friend) to Jesus's mother. Women probably looked up to her as someone to mirror.

Even though she was seen as a godly woman, she was not accepted in society because she was barren. This had to be extremely difficult for her. To be so honored by God, to be knowledgeable of God-fearing rituals, but to not be blessed with a child. She had to wait many years (most scholars say eighty-eight) to become a mother. What patience she must have had. I wonder if she was always patient.

I wonder what went through her mind when Zachariah came home for sacrificing in the temple as a mute. What crossed her mind when he told her what had happened? I wonder what questions she had? How hard it would have been for her to understand everything that had occurred and what was to occur, since her husband could not speak.

And then once he was born, scripture does not give us a time-line, but we know John lived most of his years wandering in the desert. This would have been even harder for her. To let her child go, trusting that God was in control and would keep him safe.

What we can learn from Elizabeth:

1. Elizabeth was a godly woman.

   > "Both of them were righteous in the sight of God, observing all
   > the Lord's commands and decrees blamelessly." (Luke 1:6)

2. Elizabeth had patience with God as she waited for a child.

   > "But they were childless because Elizabeth was not able to
   > conceive, and they were both very old." (Luke 1:7)

3. Elizabeth experienced the Holy Spirit herself and then was able to see Him in her husband.

> "When Elizabeth heard Mary's greeting, the baby leaped in her womb, and Elizabeth was filled with the Holy Spirit." (Luke 1:41)

Chapter 8

Mary, Mother of Jesus

Mary was just a humble, young girl from Nazareth. Nazareth was such an unknown place (see John 1:46). But this was who God chose as Jesus's earthly mother. I wonder what her childhood was like. Her lineage was from the tribe of Judah and the line of David, which was all foretold in the Old Testament. She married a man of God, Joseph, who took her as his bride even though she was pregnant. Yea, God helped with that a little. He sent a messenger, an angel. From conception to birth, Mary's pregnancy was like no other. God used little faith builders along the way to help Mary get through: Gabrielle's visit, her cousin and friend Elisabeth's support through the Holy Spirit, Joseph's dream, the timing of Jesus's birth, the angels and shepherds, His wisdom as he grew, and more. God helped Mary see that Jesus was more than just any child—He was God's child.

What we can learn from Mary:

1. God can use anybody, even a nobody.

> "For he looked on the humble estate of his servant." (Luke 1:48)

2. Mary treasured memories of her son, Jesus.

> "And Mary treasured up all these things, pondering them in her heart." (Luke 2:19)

3. Mary disciplined Jesus.

> "When his parent saw him, they were astonished. His mother said to him, 'Son, why have you treated us like this? Your father and I have been anxiously searching for you.'" (Luke 2: 48)

4. Mary was faithful to God.

> "'I am the Lord's servant,' Mary answered, 'May your
> word to me be fulfilled.'" (Luke 1:38)

5. Mary was a prayer warrior for her son.

> "They joined together constantly in prayer, along with the women and
> Mary the mother of Jesus, and with his brothers." (Acts 1:14)

Endnotes

i   "Denomination". Meriam-Webster, Incorporated. July 8, 2019. https://www.merriam-webster.com/dictionary/denomination.

ii "Religion" Meriam-Webster, Incorporated. July 8, 2019. https://www.merriam-webster.com/dictionary/religion.

iii "Relationship" Meriam-Webster, Incorporated. July 8, 2019. https://www.merriam-webster.com/dictionary/relationship.

iv "Blue Letter Bible". https://www.blueletterbible.org/.

v   "The four types of LOVE in the Bible". Foundation of life. July,8 2019. http://fountainoflifetm.com/articles/the-four-types-of-love-in-the-bible/

vi "The four types of LOVE in the Bible". Foundation of life. July,8 2019. http://fountainoflifetm.com/articles/the-four-types-of-love-in-the-bible/

vii "The four types of LOVE in the Bible". Foundation of life. July,8 2019. http://fountainoflifetm.com/articles/the-four-types-of-love-in-the-bible/

viii "The four types of LOVE in the Bible". Foundation of life. July,8 2019. http://fountainoflifetm.com/articles/the-four-types-of-love-in-the-bible/

ix Ephesians 6::King James Version. 2019 Blue Letter Bible. July 8, 2019. https://www.blueletterbible.org/kjv/eph/6/18/t_conc_1103018

x   Ephesians 6::King James Version. 2019 Blue Letter Bible. July 8, 2019. https://www.blueletterbible.org/kjv/eph/6/18/t_conc_1103018

About the Author

Let me introduce myself. My husband, Curt, and I have been married for twenty-two years. We have three amazing children; live on a farm with lots of different animals; love our outside dog, Sadie; and spoil our inside dog, Opal. We have a mother-in-law suite attached to our home, where my mother-in-law lives. She has been a major blessing to our home. She helps me keep up with laundry and even does a little cooking from time to time.

I have been a middle school teacher for the past nineteen years. I love children, and I love my job. As the years go by, I am saddened by the changes I see in our children and in education. Educational expectations have driven so many children into believing they have no value or worth. With so many dysfunctional families, I have seen a decline in respect given to the teacher by students and parents. My job has become more difficult each year. I continue to remain teaching only because God has not told me it's time to move on. But my heart is becoming heavy.

My husband is a full-time farmer. However, that has not always been his occupation. When Curt and I first me and for the beginning of our marriage, Curt worked in a factory. He made excellent money, usually worked first shift, and was able to keep the job at work. He didn't come home frustrated from the day's activities. It seemed perfect. We had money, time, and lots of love. His father, a full-time farmer, became ill. Curt had to start helping him on the farm after working in the factory all day. We lived about twenty minutes from the farm. We had no children at the time. Adding this extra work to our daily load didn't cause much stress to our lives. I just spent more time with his family and riding in tractors or trucks with my man. Curt's dad continued to decline in health, and Curt had to spend more and more time on the farm. We soon discovered that the twenty-minute drive was too much.

We began looking for a house closer to the farm. We also decided that this would be a good time to start having children. This added lots of stress as we began to fight over time and how exactly we would make these changes work in our life. Eventually we moved closer and I became pregnant. Thirteen weeks into my pregnancy, our baby's heartbeat stopped. We were at the doctor's office, so excited to finally see our baby on the ultrasound screen. But our joy quickly turned into sorrow. Our doctor ordered a D and C (dilation and curettage) surgery. I could not remove my child from my body so quickly. So she moved the surgery five days away. Two days after my doctor's appointment, I went into labor. With this being my first pregnancy, I had no idea what was happening. My husband called my best friend, who was a nurse. She and Curt drove me to the hospital, where my OBGYN was called and removed my precious child from my body. This whole experience rates as one of the worst experiences in my life. This experience set a spiral of emotional unbalance for me. Within six months, I was pregnant again. I lived in fear every day, wondering if God would choose to take this child from me too. I had started my job as seventh grade teacher. I used my job to keep me busy—a distraction from my worries. Nine months (and two weeks) later, I delivered my beautiful daughter, Kaytlin. Two years later I had Noah. Two years after Noah, I experienced another miscarriage. This time my baby lived nine weeks in my womb. I knew before the doctors even told me the heartbeat was gone. Just a mother's instinct, I guess. One year later I had my youngest, Caleb. My emotional anxiety remained unbalanced for a large majority of this time in my life. Many stories of my behavior and reactions toward my children are shared in this book. My reactions were many times blown out of proportion, as I tried to understand life through a foggy lens. This is something many women go through, and the best way to handle ourselves during these times is to learn from one another.

Our oldest, Kaytlin, turned eighteen this year. She is beyond ready to graduate from high school. She has decided to pursue her own business as a photographer. I am excited to see where God will take her. Our middle child, Noah, turned sixteen this year. We now have four drivers in our household. He helps his dad on the farm. He has also started his own cattle and rabbit business. He has both animals in the barn and spends a majority of his time there. He enjoys anything that is outdoors. Caleb is the youngest and the comedian of the gang. He is twelve years old with a heart of gold. He will talk to anyone who will listen about anything they'll listen to. He can spin a yarn no matter who, when, or where. His laughter rings through our house daily.

Throughout this book series you are going to learn a lot more about me and my family. I was not always the best mom or wife. I have made mistakes along the way. Hindsight is always twenty-twenty. I pray that my triumphs and failures may be lessons you can learn from.

Printed in the United States
By Bookmasters